THIS COUPON IS GOOD FOR

_____

_____

....

DATE REDEEMED   SIGNATURE

NO EXPIRATION. REDEEM THIS COUPON ANYTIME.

MW00952403

WITH LOVE

FROM

TO

THIS COUPON IS GOOD FOR

_____

_____

DATE REDEEMED · SIGNATURE

NO EXPIRATION. REDEEM THIS COUPON ANYTIME.

WITH LOVE

FROM

_____

TO

THIS COUPON IS GOOD FOR

_____

_____

DATE REDEEMED   SIGNATURE

NO EXPIRATION. REDEEM THIS COUPON ANYTIME.

WITH LOVE

FROM

TO

THIS COUPON IS GOOD FOR

_____

_____

DATE REDEEMED   SIGNATURE

NO EXPIRATION. REDEEM THIS COUPON ANYTIME.

WITH LOVE

FROM

TO

THIS COUPON IS GOOD FOR

_____

_____

DATE REDEEMED   SIGNATURE

NO EXPIRATION. REDEEM THIS COUPON ANYTIME.

WITH LOVE

FROM

TO

THIS COUPON IS GOOD FOR

_____

_____

DATE REDEEMED   SIGNATURE

NO EXPIRATION. REDEEM THIS COUPON ANYTIME.

WITH LOVE

FROM

_____

TO

THIS COUPON IS GOOD FOR

_____

_____

DATE REDEEMED

SIGNATURE

NO EXPIRATION. REDEEM THIS COUPON ANYTIME.

WITH LOVE

FROM

TO

THIS COUPON IS GOOD FOR

DATE REDEEMED

SIGNATURE

NO EXPIRATION. REDEEM THIS COUPON ANYTIME.

WITH LOVE

FROM

TO

THIS COUPON IS GOOD FOR

_____

_____

DATE REDEEMED   SIGNATURE

NO EXPIRATION. REDEEM THIS COUPON ANYTIME.

WITH LOVE

FROM

_____

TO

_____

THIS COUPON IS GOOD FOR

_____

_____

DATE REDEEMED   SIGNATURE

NO EXPIRATION. REDEEM THIS COUPON ANYTIME.

WITH LOVE

FROM

_____

TO

THIS COUPON IS GOOD FOR

_____

_____

DATE REDEEMED   SIGNATURE

NO EXPIRATION. REDEEM THIS COUPON ANYTIME.

WITH LOVE

FROM

TO

THIS COUPON IS GOOD FOR

_____

_____

DATE REDEEMED   SIGNATURE

NO EXPIRATION. REDEEM THIS COUPON ANYTIME.

WITH LOVE

FROM

_____

TO

_____

THIS COUPON IS GOOD FOR

_____

_____

WITH LOVE

FROM

TO

THIS COUPON IS GOOD FOR

_____

_____

DATE REDEEMED   SIGNATURE

NO EXPIRATION. REDEEM THIS COUPON ANYTIME.

WITH LOVE

FROM

TO

THIS COUPON IS GOOD FOR

_____

_____

DATE REDEEMED   SIGNATURE

NO EXPIRATION. REDEEM THIS COUPON ANYTIME.

WITH LOVE

FROM

_____

TO

THIS COUPON IS GOOD FOR

_____

_____

_____   _____
DATE REDEEMED   SIGNATURE

NO EXPIRATION. REDEEM THIS COUPON ANYTIME.

WITH LOVE

FROM

TO

THIS COUPON IS GOOD FOR

DATE REDEEMED

SIGNATURE

NO EXPIRATION. REDEEM THIS COUPON ANYTIME.

WITH LOVE

FROM

TO

THIS COUPON IS GOOD FOR

_____

_____

DATE REDEEMED   SIGNATURE

NO EXPIRATION. REDEEM THIS COUPON ANYTIME.

WITH LOVE

FROM

TO

THIS COUPON IS GOOD FOR

_____

_____

DATE REDEEMED   SIGNATURE

NO EXPIRATION. REDEEM THIS COUPON ANYTIME.

WITH LOVE

FROM

_____

TO

THIS COUPON IS GOOD FOR

_____

_____

DATE REDEEMED   SIGNATURE

NO EXPIRATION. REDEEM THIS COUPON ANYTIME.

WITH LOVE

FROM

_____

TO

THIS COUPON IS GOOD FOR

_____

_____

DATE REDEEMED   SIGNATURE

NO EXPIRATION. REDEEM THIS COUPON ANYTIME.

WITH LOVE

FROM

_____

TO

THIS COUPON IS GOOD FOR

_____

_____

DATE REDEEMED   SIGNATURE

NO EXPIRATION. REDEEM THIS COUPON ANYTIME.

WITH LOVE

FROM

TO

THIS COUPON IS GOOD FOR

DATE REDEEMED

SIGNATURE

NO EXPIRATION. REDEEM THIS COUPON ANYTIME.

WITH LOVE

FROM

_____

TO

THIS COUPON IS GOOD FOR

DATE REDEEMED   SIGNATURE

NO EXPIRATION. REDEEM THIS COUPON ANYTIME.

WITH LOVE

FROM

TO

THIS COUPON IS GOOD FOR

_____

_____

DATE REDEEMED   SIGNATURE

NO EXPIRATION. REDEEM THIS COUPON ANYTIME.

WITH LOVE

FROM

_____

TO

_____

THIS COUPON IS GOOD FOR

_____

_____

DATE REDEEMED   SIGNATURE

NO EXPIRATION. REDEEM THIS COUPON ANYTIME.

WITH LOVE

FROM

_____

TO

THIS COUPON IS GOOD FOR

_____

_____

DATE REDEEMED   SIGNATURE

NO EXPIRATION. REDEEM THIS COUPON ANYTIME.

WITH LOVE

FROM

TO

THIS COUPON IS GOOD FOR

_____

_____

DATE REDEEMED   SIGNATURE

NO EXPIRATION. REDEEM THIS COUPON ANYTIME.

WITH LOVE

FROM

TO

THIS COUPON IS GOOD FOR

_____

_____

DATE REDEEMED   SIGNATURE

NO EXPIRATION. REDEEM THIS COUPON ANYTIME.

WITH LOVE

FROM

TO

THIS COUPON IS GOOD FOR

_____

_____

DATE REDEEMED   SIGNATURE

NO EXPIRATION. REDEEM THIS COUPON ANYTIME.

WITH LOVE

FROM

_____

TO

Made in the USA
Monee, IL
05 December 2024